What's the Issue?

WHAT'S ARTIFICIAL INTELLIGENCE?

By Judy Thorpe

KidHaven
PUBLISHING

Published in 2025 by
KidHaven Publishing, an Imprint of Greenhaven Publishing, LLC
2544 Clinton Street
Buffalo, NY 14224

Designer: Deanna Lepovich
Editor: Jennifer Lombardo

Photo credits: Cover (top) ImYanis/Shutterstock.com; cover (bottom) Suwin/Shutterstock.com; p. 5 Antlii/Shutterstock.com; p. 7 Andriy Blokhin/Shutterstock.com; p. 9 JCDH/Shutterstock.com; p. 11 seewhatmitchsee/Shutterstock.com; p. 15 Shutterstock.AI/Shutterstock.com; p. 17 Stefano Mazzola/Shutterstock.com; p. 19 VesnaArt/Shutterstock.com; p. 21 fuad_vector/Shutterstock.com.

Cataloging-in-Publication Data

Names: Thorpe, Judy.
Title: What's artificial intelligence? / Judy Thorpe.
Description: Buffalo, New York : KidHaven Publishing, 2025. | Series: What's the issue? | Includes glossary and index.
Identifiers: ISBN 9781534547971 (pbk.) | ISBN 9781534547988 (library bound) | ISBN 9781534547995 (ebook)
Subjects: LCSH: Artificial intelligence–Juvenile literature. | Artificial intelligence–Industrial applications–Juvenile literature. | Technology–Juvenile literature.
Classification: LCC Q335.4 T56 2025 | DDC 006.3–dc23

Printed in the United States of America

Some of the images in this book illustrate individuals who are models. The depictions do not imply actual situations or events.

CPSIA compliance information: Batch #CSKH25: For further information contact Greenhaven Publishing LLC at 1-844-317-7404.

Please visit our website, www.greenhavenpublishing.com. For a free color catalog of all our high-quality books, call toll free 1-844-317-7404 or fax 1-844-317-7405.

Find us on

CONTENTS

Fake but Smart

"Artificial intelligence," or AI, **describes** a machine's ability to seemingly think like a human. There are many different forms of AI. Some are simple, while others are very **complex**. You might not realize it, but a lot of the machines around you use some form of AI!

Have you ever asked Siri or Google to do something for you? Does Netflix or Disney+ suggest shows you might like? Those are both examples of ways people use AI in their everyday life. Every day, people are working on making AI even smarter and more helpful.

Facing the Facts

"Artificial" means made by people. "Intelligence" is a measure of how smart someone or something is.

AI helps make phones easier to use.

A Short History of AI

Computers have been around since the 1800s, but they didn't look or act anything like they do today. Over the years, scientists have worked on ways to make computers better at storing and **retrieving** information.

In the 1950s, a computer scientist named Arthur Samuel created a computer program that used AI to play checkers. In 1962, the computer beat the world's best checkers player. Since then, people have used AI to make cars that drive themselves, robots that talk like humans, washing machines that send a text when clothes are clean, and much more.

Facing the Facts

The Turing test was named after a computer scientist named Alan Turing. It tests whether AI is as intelligent and **self-aware** as a human.

This robot uses AI to check the **inventory** at a store.

Machine Learning

Arthur Samuel's checkers program worked by using machine learning. This is when a computer **analyzes** information from the past and uses that information to change what it does in the **future**. The checkers program analyzed past games, noticed what it did wrong, and then made different moves in future games.

AI can use machine learning in other ways that help humans. For example, a Roomba is a kind of robotic vacuum, or cleaning machine. It uses machine learning to figure out the best way to vacuum a room. Over time, it learns how to stay away from things that shouldn't be vacuumed, like computer cords.

Facing the Facts

All machine-learning tools are examples of AI. However, not all AI uses machine learning to work.

A Roomba can be turned on with a person's phone. It vacuums on its own and learns over time what should be vacuumed and what should be left alone.

AI All Around

More and more, AI is used to help people in big and small ways. Machine learning helps AI predict, or guess, things based on past events. For example, AI can help predict when flu season will start. This lets health-care workers have enough flu shots ready for when they need them.

People can use AI to control their smart **devices** even when they aren't home. With an app on their phone or a device such as a Google Home or an Amazon Echo, a person may be able to control the lights, heat, and other things in their house just by speaking or pushing a button.

Facing the Facts

AI has made a lot of things much easier. For example, AI can tell farmers the best time to plant their crops by analyzing past growing seasons.

Many people have an Amazon Echo in their home. They can use this device to ask Alexa, Amazon's voice service, to tell them things or do things for them.

Good or Bad?

Some people love the ways AI helps make life easier for humans. AI can "think" for itself, so it saves people a lot of time at their jobs and at home. Computers also don't make as many mistakes as humans do. They don't get tired or hurt, so they can do jobs that are dangerous, or unsafe, for humans.

Other people think AI itself is dangerous and could become too powerful. They worry that AI will take jobs away from humans. They also worry about AI sharing their private information.

Facing the Facts

Some AI tools can quickly look up information and give people answers. This can be helpful in some jobs. However, people worry that this will make it too easy for students to cheat on tests and homework.

Growing Concern

% of U.S. adults who say the increased use of artificial intelligence in daily life makes them feel...

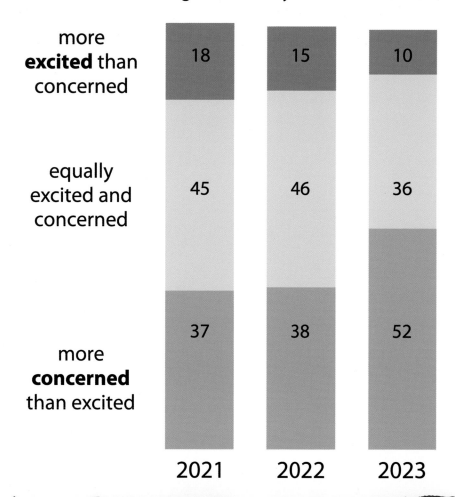

more **excited** than concerned: 18 (2021), 15 (2022), 10 (2023)

equally excited and concerned: 45 (2021), 46 (2022), 36 (2023)

more **concerned** than excited: 37 (2021), 38 (2022), 52 (2023)

In the last few years, people have gotten less excited and more worried about the use of AI in daily life, as this information from Pew Research Center shows.

Art and Writing

Around 2022, AI programs that can create art and writing started to become very popular. A person gives a prompt, or idea, to the AI program. Then, the program generates, or creates, art or writing from that prompt. Sometimes what it generates is very good. Other times, it's not as good as something a human could make.

Some people think generative AI is a lot of fun. Other people say we shouldn't use it. A big problem with generative AI is that it copies human creators without their permission. People also worry that human artists and writers will lose their jobs because AI is cheaper to use.

Facing the Facts

Hollywood writers and actors went on strike, or stopped working, in 2023. One reason they went on strike was because they were worried about movie and TV studios using AI—especially without their permission.

AI art programs often have trouble making hands that look real.

15

What Can It Do?

If an AI program is given the right information, or data, by humans, it can improve the way people do things. For example, information about how many cars are on the road at certain times of day can help AI programs decide when a traffic light should change color.

AI can also be used to explain complex ideas in a simple way. It can give a recipe based on what someone has in their fridge. Robots that use AI can take a pile of many items and sort those items into piles. These are only a few of the many things AI can do.

Facing the Facts

AI has become such a common part of our world that most people don't realize how much they use it. As AI gets better, it will likely become an even bigger part of our lives.

These robot servers use AI to bring
the right food to the right table.

What Can't It Do?

Many people think AI is more powerful than it really is. AI can't read your mind. It can guess at what will happen in the future, but it can't know exactly what will happen. AI also doesn't have feelings. It can pretend to care about people, but it can't feel love or **empathy**.

Some people worry that AI will take over the world someday. However, it doesn't have the right tools to do that. It can't solve, or fix, problems it doesn't already have information about. AI can only work when humans are running it.

Facing the Facts

When scientists create something new, they need to think about the **ethics** of what they're doing. Some people think it's unethical to create a machine that's just like a human if we aren't going to treat it like a person.

Some people think robots will one day be able to think and act just like humans. However, it's unlikely this will ever happen. If it does, it's many years away from happening.

19

Taking Action

Whether people like or dislike AI, the fact is that it's here to stay. It's already so much a part of our lives that it would be nearly impossible to go back to the way life was before.

It's important to remember that we can only get out of AI what we put into it. AI isn't good or bad on its own, but it can be used in ways that are good or bad. The question we need to ask isn't "Should we use AI?" Instead, it's "What are the most useful and ethical ways to use AI?"

Facing the Facts

AI doesn't have feelings, so many people think it can't be **biased**. However, an AI program can be biased if the information it's given has a bias. This could cause it to make choices that accidentally hurt people.

WHAT CAN YOU DO?

Let AI creators know that you want their AI to be unbiased, safe, and ethical.

Learn about coding and computers if you want to get a job working with AI in the future.

If you feel strongly that there should be laws about AI, write to government leaders.

Think about how you can use AI in the most ethical way.

Talk to trusted adults about the good and bad of AI.

Learn more about the ways AI affects your daily life, both directly and indirectly.

Learning more about AI is the first step toward knowing how to use it in ethical ways.

GLOSSARY

analyze: To study something closely.

biased: Having an unfair preference for or dislike of something.

complex: Having to do with something with many parts that work together.

describe: To represent or give an account of in words.

device: A tool or machine made to perform a task.

empathy: The ability to be aware of and share a person's feelings and experiences.

ethics: A set of issues that deal with doing the right thing.

future: What is going to happen.

inventory: The stock of goods on hand.

retrieve: To get back again.

self-aware: Having an understanding of who and what one is.

FOR MORE INFORMATION

WEBSITES

ChatGPT

chat.openai.org

Ask a trusted adult to help you have a conversation with ChatGPT—an AI program.

Kiddle: Artificial Intelligence Facts for Kids

kids.kiddle.co/Artificial_intelligence

Learn more about the past, present, and future of AI.

BOOKS

Jackson, Tom. *Artificial Intelligence*. New York, NY: Kingfisher, 2022.

Kulz, George Anthony. *Artificial Intelligence in the Real World*. Lake Elmo, MN: Focus Readers, 2020.

Williams, Dinah. *Artificial Intelligence*. New York, NY: Starry Forest Books, 2021.

INDEX